musical by

Jimmy Travis Getzen *and* Gail Getzen

arranged by

Tim Hayden *and* Jimmy Travis Getzen

produced by

Jimmy Travis Getzen *and* Gail Getzen

PRODUCTS AVAILABLE

*Listening CDs are available at a reduced rate when bought in quantities of 10 or more.

0-6331-9825-0

A WORD FROM THE WRITERS

Welcome to a STOMP-endous adventure!

What a world in which we live! Our kids are besieged with mixed messages about life and truth. How will they know if what they see on TV, watch at the movies, and hear in music is of the world or of God?

They need to see for themselves what God's Word says. But in this fast-paced, media-driven world, how do we hold their attention long enough to teach them God's Truth?—with STOMP! What kid does not want to beat on pots and pans, or drum on a trash can? Stomp music is high energy, fun, and has a unique appeal to kids of all ages.

Now that we have their attention, what do we teach them? We teach them about the godly character the Lord wants to develop in each of us—integrity, faith, courage, endurance, humility, compassion, and forgiveness. All of these are seen in Joseph's life. We teach them that they can trust God because He is all-powerful, all-knowing, and in control of everything that happens. They see this lived out in Joseph's life.

Joseph: From the Pit to the Palace is upbeat and fun. It is easy to learn and simple to produce, allowing more time to have fun with the Stomp. Joseph's story is told in a *This Is Your Life* setting. Costumes are minimal and donned onstage before the audience. This is a unique musical that will keep every kid engaged—even the older ones!

We know this will be an exciting time for your choir. We pray that the truths your kids learn from Joseph's life will change them forever!

Have fun, and rock on!

May God be glorified!

Jimmy & Gail Getzen

Joseph's story is found in Genesis 37–50. Our musical covers Genesis 37, 39–46.

SEQUENCE

*(When choir and stomp players are in place, **Joseph-1** and **Em-shee** move downstage center to deliver opening lines. Everyone is in "Stomp" attire.)*

Joseph-1:   Welcome, everyone! Tonight's going to be exciting because we're celebrating the life of Joseph!

(Everyone cheers and applauds.)

Em-shee: Even though Joseph lived almost four thousand years ago, his life shows us how we should live today.

Joseph-1:   Joseph knew God and trusted Him. And in Joseph's life, we see the godly character that the Lord wants to develop in all of us.

Em-shee: Tonight, we want you to be a part of this STOMP-endous celebration, so check the screens for your cues! Hold on to your seats—watch, listen, and learn as Joseph goes from the pit to the palace!

(Everyone cheers and applauds.)

Joseph

Words and Music by
JIMMY TRAVIS GETZEN

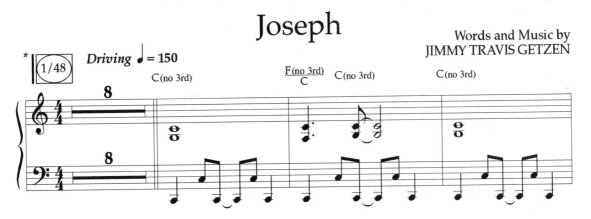

*These numbers refer to the Accompaniment CD. The first set of numbers is for the reference points related to the split-track versions of the product. The second set of numbers is for the stereo tracks (instruments only).

5/52

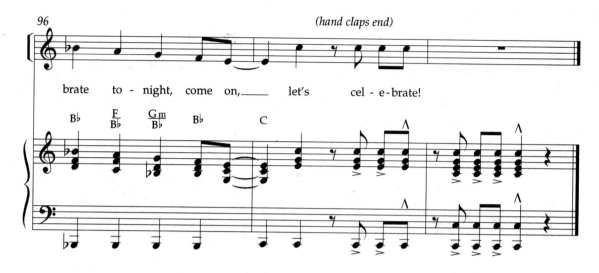

brate to - night, come on,___ let's cel - e - brate!

(As song begins, **Em-shee** and **Joseph-1** move to prop table. They add costume pieces over their "Stomp" attire, gather props, and take their places stage right. **Joseph** is seated in "chair of honor.")

>   **Em-shee:** Joseph, this is your life! *(opens book)*

(Everyone cheers and applauds, continuing as Fanfare is played.)

(7/54) Stomp Fanfare sound effect

>   **Em-shee:** *(refers to book as she speaks)* You grew up in the land of Canaan with your father, Jacob, and your 11 brothers—you were the second youngest. Tonight, we have some special people from your past who have come to help us celebrate. See if you recognize this voice!

>   **Bilhah:** *(spoken from behind screen or offstage)* You were such a cute little boy, and your father loved you so much! He had big plans for your life and made a special coat just for you.

>   **Joseph-1:** Why, that's Bilhah—our housekeeper!

(As Intro to song begins, **Bilhah** enters to sing solo.)

One Good Lookin' Hebrew

Words and Music by
JIMMY TRAVIS GETZEN

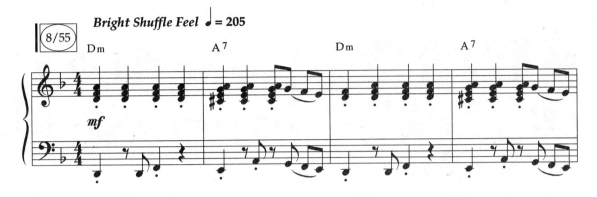

(Coat Carriers *enter at measure 21. They dance with the coat, then put it on* **Joseph-1.)**

Joseph-1: This looks just like my old coat. I loved that coat, but it sure caused a lot of problems with my brothers.

Em-shee: You can say that again. And when you were 17 years old, your life was turned upside down. See if this brings back memories. *(gestures toward center stage)*

DRAMA 1 SEGUE
Drama 1: "A 'Pitiful' Situation"

(As music begins, **Sign Bearers** *enter with sign 1. They cross downstage left to right, showing sign to audience, then exit. As sign is shown, Drama 1 cast moves to prop table to put on costume pieces and get props. They take their places center stage. Dialogue begins after* **Sign Bearers** *exit.)*

Brother 1: Oh, great! Look who's coming. You can see that tacky coat for miles!

Reuben: It looks like it should be seat covers on a chariot!

Judah: I can't stand him. It's bad enough he's our father's favorite and will one day be the head of the family, but now all we hear about are those crazy dreams of his, where he sees us all bowing down to him.

Brother 1: That'll never happen!

Reuben: I've had about enough of him.

Brother 1: I hate him!

Brother 2: Come on, let's kill him. Let's get rid of him for good!

Judah: But what are we going to tell our father?

Brother 2: Uhmm...tell him an animal ate him.

Reuben: No, no! Don't kill him! Just throw him into one of the pits.

Brother 1: That's a great idea! Consider it done! Then we'll see what becomes of his dreams.

*(**Brothers** ad-lib:Yeah. Good riddance. Great idea.That's perfect.)*

*(**Reuben** and **Brother I** exit.)*

Judah:	*(pointing offstage)* Hey, guys, look over there! What do you see?
Brother 2:	I see a caravan heading our way. What do you see?
Judah:	I see opportunity knocking! That's a group of Ishmaelites going to Egypt to do some trading. Have I got a deal for them! If we let Joseph die in that pit, what's in it for us?
All Brothers:	Nothing!
Judah:	Let's sell him to the Ishmaelites and make a little money.
Brother 2:	He'll be going, going, gone forever!

*(**Auctioneer** moves downstage. Prearranged bids come from audience.)*

Going, Going, Gone

Words and Music by
JIMMY TRAVIS GETZEN

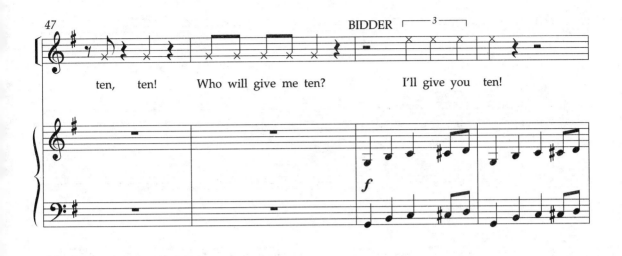

BIDDER

ten,   ten!   Who will give me ten?   I'll give you   ten!

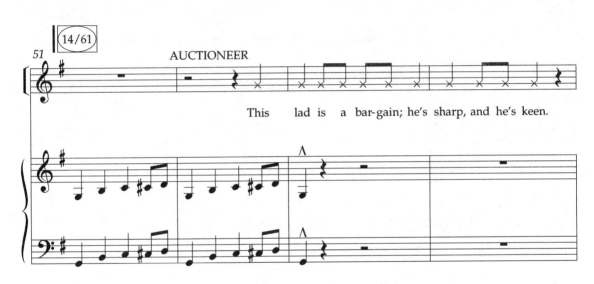

14/61

AUCTIONEER

This   lad is   a bar-gain; he's sharp, and he's keen.

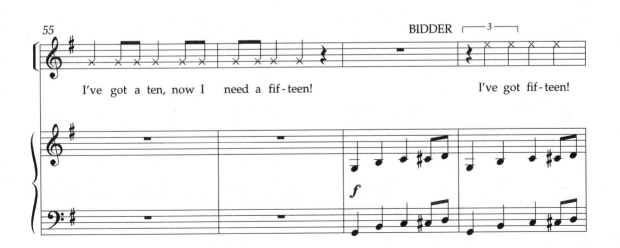

BIDDER

I've got a ten, now I   need a fif-teen!   I've got fif-teen!

Em-shee: Joseph, I can't imagine going through something like that. Weren't you scared? Didn't you feel hurt, and alone?

Joseph-1: Yeah, it was the pits! *(allow time for laughter)* But God's always faithful, and He helped me. When you're going through tough times, you just have to remember that God's in control of everything that happens. He knows what you're going through. And you really aren't alone because God is right there with you. Just trust Him, and He'll help you through your "pitiful" situation. *(making quotation mark motions with fingers as "pitiful" is spoken)*

It's the Pits

Words and Music by
JIMMY TRAVIS GETZEN

feel-ing down with no friends a-round,__ it's the pits.

18/65

CHOIR *mf*

No one to talk to,__ all by your-

G(no 3rd)　　　　　　A(no 3rd)

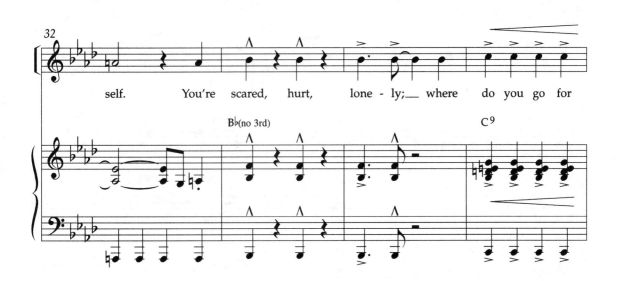

self. You're scared, hurt, lone-ly;__ where do you go for

B♭(no 3rd)　　　　　　C⁹

help? It's the pits. It's the pits.

When you're real-ly dumb-found-ed and your trou-bles are com-pound-ed, it's the pits.

It's the pits.

It's the pits.

When you're down___ just look up, 'cause God is in con-trol.

34

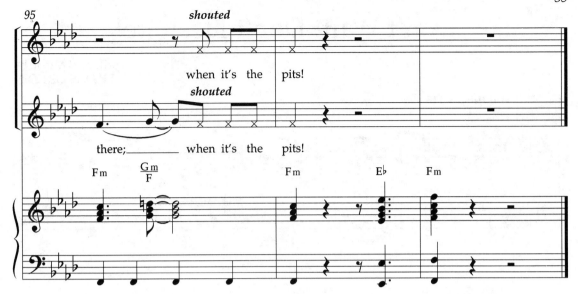

Em-shee: Joseph, when you got to Egypt, our next guest bought you from the Ishmaelite traders.

Joseph-1: Oh, you're talking about Potiphar—Pharaoh's captain of the guard.

Em-shee: That's right!

(Potiphar enters.)

Potiphar: Joseph, you became a trusted servant in my house. I could tell that God was with you because He made everything you did successful! I'm no dummy; I put you in charge of my household and fields. Because of you, God blessed all that I owned.

Everything was fine until my wife tried to get you to sin. But you were a man of integrity and obeyed God's laws.

Em-shee: Joseph, you did the right thing!

Joseph-1: Well, it was God that gave me the strength to stand up to the temptation. He always gives us a way out when we're faced with sin. It's up to us to choose His way.

Em-shee: And that's what you did. You didn't think twice; you knew just what to do!

Don't Wait! Don't Hesitate!

Words and Music by
JIMMY TRAVIS GETZEN

When you find your-self in a

sit-u-a-tion that is not right, full

23/70 *1st time*
26/73 *2nd time*

take con-trol of the sit-u-a-tion.

Ex - it, leave, e - vac - u - ate. Hit the road,_ don't hes - i - tate._ When

things aren't right and sin is close, give 'em a great big "A-di-os."_ Don't

2nd time to Coda (meas. 37)

shout · sing (opt. ensemble) · shout

wait. Don't hes-i-tate. Don't wait. Don't hes-i-tate.

But

folks tell you, "Hey, it's all right.

Ev-'ry-bod-y's do-in' it, so give it a try."

Em-shee: *(looks at book)* Even though you had done nothing wrong, Potiphar believed his wife's lies and sent you to prison. You were there a long time, but you had courage and endurance. God kept blessing you, and soon you were in charge of all that went on in the prison. That's when you met two very interesting people!

Joseph-1: Ohhh, that would be Pharaoh's cupbearer and baker. When we were in prison together, they had strange dreams, and God gave me the meaning of the dreams.

Em-shee: And two years later, Pharaoh had strange dreams. Remember this? *(gestures toward center stage)*

DRAMA 2 SEGUE
Drama 2: "I've Got Good News and Bad News"

(As segue music begins, **Sign Bearers** *enter with sign 2. They cross downstage left to right, showing sign to audience, then exit. As sign is shown, Drama 2 cast moves to prop table to put on costume pieces and get props.* **Pharaoh, Cupbearer,** *and optional* **Attendants** *take their places center stage.* **Attendants** *stand on either side of* **Pharaoh,** *slightly upstage.* **Cupbearer** *stands upstage right of* **Pharaoh** *until he steps forward to deliver his lines. Dialogue begins after* **Sign Bearers** *exit.)*

Pharaoh: I would not, could not understand
My two dreams, so I command
That someone tell me what they mean,
These seven fat cows and seven lean.

Inform me now, who will explain
About the fourteen heads of grain,
With seven good and seven burned,
The meaning of which I should learn.

Cupbearer: I know a man, I do, oh, King,
Who through his God interprets dreams.
I would not, should not have forgotten
About this man, and I feel rotten.

His name is Joseph, this hip Hebrew,
He'll be here soon to speak with you.
His God will help him to explain
All about the cows and grain.

(**Joseph-2** *moves to stage left side of* **Pharaoh**.)

Joseph-2: Greetings, Pharaoh, and hear these things
God has told me about your dreams.
Know these words from God are true,
For He's revealed what He's about to do.

The cows and grain, here's what they mean:
Seven years of plenty and seven of lean.
The abundant years will produce great crops,
But when the famine comes all that stops.

So find a wise and discerning man;
Put him in charge of Egypt land.
For seven years store up grain,
And you'll have food when famine reigns.

Pharaoh: I would not, could not, yes, it's true,
Find one better than this Hebrew.
For you're a strong and godly man,
You're now in charge of Pharaoh's land!

(*Everyone applauds.*)

Joseph-1: (*nodding, applauding, chuckling*) Very clever. I would not, could not, have done it better!

Em-shee: Joseph, when you were 30 years old, you got a big promotion. You went from the pit to the palace and became second in command of all Egypt. How did you remain so humble?

Joseph-1: People tried to give me credit for interpreting the dreams and storing the grain. But it wasn't from me; it was all from God. God knows all things, even the future. He knew the famine was coming, and He provided a way for people to survive it. I'm just honored that God let me be a part of His plan. He deserves all the glory. It's not about me; it's all about Him.

It's Not About Me

Words and Music by
JIMMY TRAVIS GETZEN

must de - crease. All my - self__ I put__ a - side.__

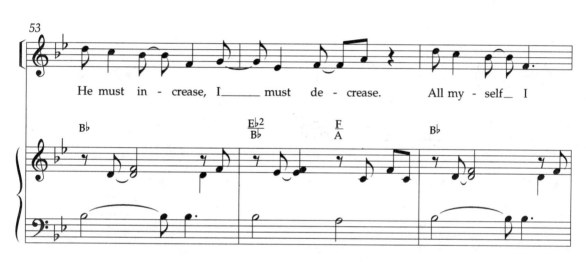

He must in - crease, I____ must de - crease. All my - self__ I

put a - side.__ He must in - crease, I____

CHOIR 2

It's not a - bout me.

48

Em-shee: Everything God said came true. There were seven years with great crops, and then the seven years of famine started. It was terrible, and soon people from other countries came to Egypt to buy the grain you had stored. This brought some very interesting visitors. *(gestures toward center stage)*

 DRAMA 3 SEGUE
Drama 3: "Long Time, No See"

*(As music begins, **Sign Bearers** enter with sign 3. They cross downstage left to right, showing sign to audience, then exit. As sign is shown, Drama 3 cast moves to prop table to put on costume pieces and get props. **Attendants** and **Joseph-2** take their places center stage. **Attendants** stand on either side of **Joseph-2** and slightly upstage. As **Sign Bearers** exit, **Joseph-2** and **Attendants** confer; the **Brothers** enter and bow before him with their faces to the ground. They are stage left of **Joseph-2**.)*

*(**Joseph-2** moves slightly downstage to deliver his aside, then returns to drama cast. Remaining Drama 3 cast freezes during aside; unfreezes when **Joseph-2** speaks to them.)*

Joseph-2: *(speaking to audience)* I can't believe it! These are my brothers! I haven't seen them in 20 years. I don't think they recognize me. And look! *(gestures to brothers)* They're bowing down to me, just like in my dreams! Let's see what they're up to. *(Returning to drama cast, he speaks forcefully to brothers.)* Stand, foreigners! Where do you come from?

Reuben: We're from the land of Canaan, sir. There's a terrible famine there, and we've come here to buy food.

Joseph-2: I think you're spies, and you've come to see the weakness of Egypt.

(All react nervously, speaking lines in quick succession.)

Simeon: No, no sir! We've only come to buy food!

Brother 1: We're honest men; we're not spies!

Brother 2: We're 12 brothers—sons of Jacob, great grandsons of Abraham. Our youngest brother is with our father, and one brother is dead.

(Joseph-2 *moves slightly downstage for aside; others freeze.)*

Joseph-2: *(speaking to audience)* Maybe my father is still alive, and my brother, Benjamin, too! Let's find out. *(Returning to drama cast, he speaks to brothers.)* Here's how you can prove you're honest men. Leave one brother here in the guardhouse, while the rest of you take grain back to Canaan to feed your families. Then, bring your youngest brother back to me; that will prove you're not spies.

*(All **Brothers** bow as they back away slightly.)*

Reuben: Thank you, sir, thank you. That's just what we'll do.

(Joseph-2 and **Attendants** *move a few steps away. They turn slightly away from* **Brothers**, *but are obviously listening to their conversation.)*

Simeon: *(speaking to **Brothers**)* We're in trouble now!

Brother 1: What a mess!

Brother 2: OK, who's going to stay here in Egypt? Any volunteers? *(All **Brothers** look at each other. **Brother 2** continues.)* No? Then let's decide like real men, "Rock, Paper, Scissors."

*(All **Brothers** do the "Rock, Paper, Scissors" game. Each **Brother** hits his fist against his palm as "Rock, paper, scissors" is spoken. On "scissors," they show rock, paper, or scissors. They repeat 3 times.)*

Reuben: Sorry, Simeon, you stay.

*(**Attendants** take **Simeon** by the arms and lead him out.)*

Brother 2: *(speaking to **Brothers**)* I can't believe this! Our father is going to be so upset when he hears that Simeon is in jail. And you know how attached he is to Benjamin; he'll never let us bring him back.

Brother 1: This is awful. Obviously, we're being punished for what we did to our brother, Joseph. He begged us not to harm him, but we wouldn't listen!

Reuben: Didn't I tell you not to hurt the boy? Now we have to pay for what we've done. This is what we deserve! It's payback time!

(Brothers exit. **Joseph-2** moves slightly downstage for aside.)

Joseph-2: (speaking to audience) I can't believe my brothers didn't recognize me. But they've changed, too; God has changed their hearts.

I Forgive

Words and Music by
JIMMY TRAVIS GETZEN

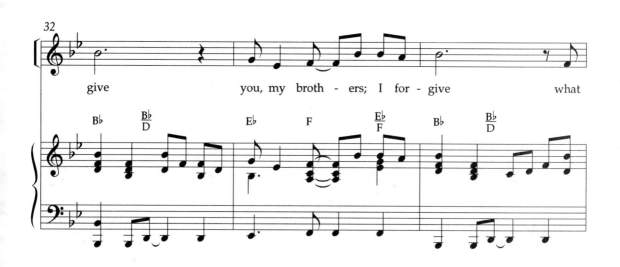

Em-shee: Joseph, may I ask you a personal question? After all that your brothers did to you, how were you able to forgive them and show them compassion?

Joseph-1: I spent a lot of time talking with God about that! He helped me forgive them. God forgives me when I sin against Him, and He expects me to forgive others when they sin against me.

Em-shee: That's hard to do.

Joseph-1: But, with God, all things are possible.

Em-shee: *(nods agreement, then looks at the book)* Well, Joseph, the famine continued and, once again, your family in Canaan ran out of food. Your father, Jacob, had no choice; he had to let your brothers take Benjamin and go back to Egypt. That's when this man became a key player.

Stew: *(speaking from offstage or behind screen)* Hello, Mr. Joseph! I know you remember me! I was your "go-to guy" during operation "Give 'em Grain."

Joseph-1: *(chuckling)* I'd know that voice anywhere; it's my steward, Stew!

(Stew enters.)

Stew: Good evening, Mr. Joseph. I'll never forget the day that your brothers returned to Egypt. As soon as you saw them, you turned to me and said, "Stew, we're throwing a party! Prepare a feast!"

Mr. Joseph, when your brothers arrived for lunch and you saw your younger brother, uh—I think he must be a musician, I believe his name was Ben-Jammin'… *(Optional: plays air guitar)*

Joseph-1: *(laughing)* It's pronounced Benjamin, Stew!

Stew: Oh, sorry, Mr. Joseph. Anyway, when you saw him, you got teary-eyed and had to leave the room. I could tell he was your favorite. When it was time for your brothers to leave for home, you had me set up a little surprise for them. Do you remember what that was, Mr. Joseph?

Joseph-1: I certainly do, Stew—"Operation Bring 'Em Back." We put the money they paid for the grain back in their sacks. And, in Benjamin's sack, we put my silver cup.

Stew: When they had gone just a short way from town, you had me go and get 'em! I had those boys open their bags, and I accused them of being thieves. Don't you know they were shocked? *(gestures to audience)*

(Audience and Choir shout, "Yes!")

Stew: Don't you know they were confused?

(Audience and Choir shout, "Yes!")

Stew: Don't you know they were scared?

(Audience and Choir shout, "Yes!")

Stew: And don't you know I loaded them up on their donkeys and trotted them right back to Mr. Joseph!

(Audience and Choir shout, "Yes!")

Em-shee: And here's what happened next! *(gestures toward center stage)*

 DRAMA 4 SEGUE MUSIC
Drama 4: "Show and Tell"

*(As music begins, **Sign Bearers** enter with sign 4. They cross downstage left to right, showing sign to audience, then exit. As sign is shown, Drama 4 cast moves to prop table to put on costume pieces and get props. **Attendants** and **Joseph-2** take their places as before. As **Sign Bearers** exit, **Brothers** enter the drama area carrying grain and moneybags. **Benjamin** carries cup. They are clearly upset and ad-lib to each other. "We didn't take the money; What's happening here? I don't understand—how did that cup get in the bag?," etc. Seeing **Joseph-2**, **Brothers** bow down to the ground before him.)*

Joseph-2: *(speaking harshly)* What were you thinking? Didn't you know you'd be caught? *(pointing to **Benjamin**)* You, with my silver cup…you will be my slave! The rest of you can go home to your father. (**Brothers** stand.)

Judah: Please, sir, please don't do this. Benjamin is our father's youngest son. It will kill him if the boy doesn't come home. Please, let me be your slave instead. Let Benjamin go home with my other brothers. It will break my father's heart if he doesn't come home.

*(**Joseph-2** moves slightly downstage for aside; others freeze.)*

Joseph-2: *(to audience)* I can't take it any longer. I've got to tell them who I am! *(Returning to drama cast, he speaks gently to **Brothers**.)* Come closer. Please, come closer! (**Brothers** move toward him.) I'm Joseph—your brother! The one you sold to the Ishmaelite traders!

*(**Brothers** react. They step back, shocked, scared, looking at each other in alarm.)*

Joseph-2: *(soothingly)* Now, don't be scared; it's OK! And don't be upset with yourselves for what you've done. Because God sent me to Egypt ahead of you, so He could keep our family alive during the famine. God put me in Egypt, not you!

*(**Brothers** speak in quick succession.)*

Benjamin: Joseph? Is it really you?

Judah: We never thought we'd see you again. It's been more than 20 years!

Brother I: You're alive! And in charge of Egypt! I can't believe it!

Joseph-2: All of this was part of God's plan. He's in control of everything. He's all-powerful, and He knows all things, including the future! He's an amazing and mighty God.

Our Mighty God

Words and Music by
JIMMY TRAVIS GETZEN

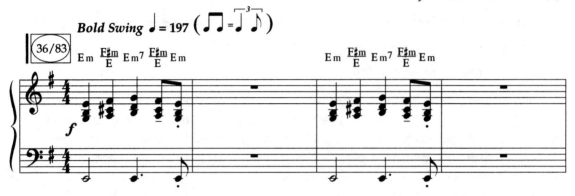

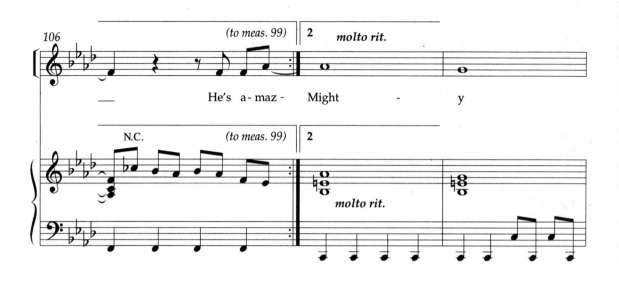

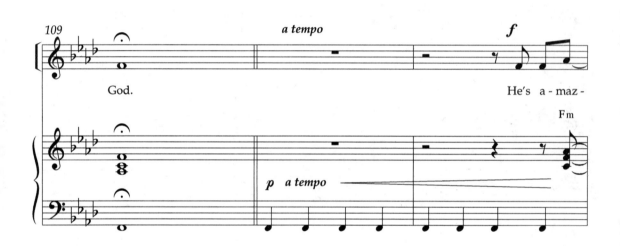

Em-shee: Joseph, we have one final chapter of your life to celebrate. We know you could never forget this voice!

Jacob: *(spoken from offstage or behind the screen)* The happiest day of my life was when your brothers came home and told me that you were alive. Our family moved to Egypt to be near you, so God could provide for us during the last five years of the famine.

Joseph-1: Of course! That's my father, Jacob. (**Jacob** *enters.*)

Jacob: Son, I was amazed when I learned all that had happened to you, and that you were second in command of Egypt. Through all your trials, you trusted God because you knew Him and understood His character. I'm so proud of the man you have become. God has truly done a great work in your life.

Joseph-1: (**Joseph** *stands.*) Thank you, Father.

(**Jacob** *nods then moves upstage so focus is on* **Joseph** *as he continues his speech.* **Joseph-1** *steps downstage or toward center.*)

70

Joseph-1: And thanks to all of you *(gesturing to* **Em-shee**, *Choir, and audience)* for this wonderful celebration tonight. But all the praise and glory should go to God! God is faithful. He was with me for each step of my journey, and He was in control of all that happened. God brought me to Egypt. God blessed me in the house of Potiphar and in prison as well. God sent Pharaoh's dreams and gave me the interpretation. God placed me in command of Egypt...all of this to accomplish His plans.

But I'm no different than you. Just as God did for me, He will see you through every circumstance that comes your way. And more than that, He will bless you, and teach you, and mold your character.

So know Him and trust Him. And, if you're willing, God will give you the privilege of being involved in His plans. He's the all-powerful, all-knowing, ever-present God. Let's praise Him now and forever.

I Just Want to Praise

Words and Music by
JIMMY TRAVIS GETZEN

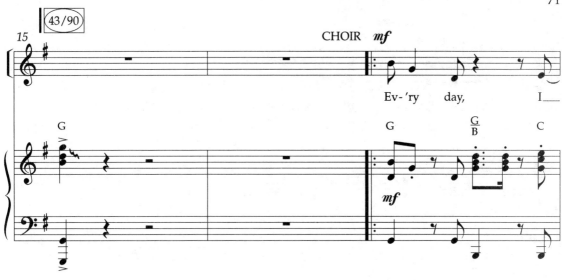

just want to praise, I____ just want to praise You, Lord.

(to meas. 17)

Lord.   You're the

One and On - ly, Ho - ly God.__ Your mer-cy en-dures for-ev -

Ev-'ry day, I_____ just want to praise, I_____ just want to praise You,

Lord.

Let the name of the Lord

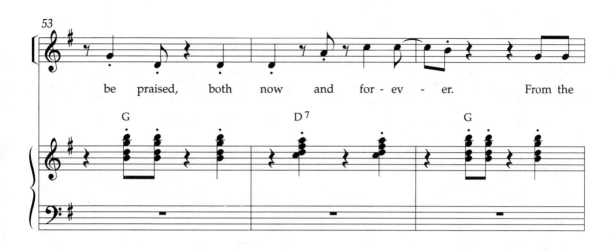

now and for - ev - er. From the ris-ing of the sun to___

Lord.___ Praise the Lord,___

___ its set - ting let the name of the Lord be praised.

(CHOIR 3 or Ens.) *f*

let the name of the Lord be praised. Praise the

CAST OF CHARACTERS

THIS IS YOUR LIFE CAST

*Note: Actors in **This Is Your Life** cast, except Joseph-1 and Em-shee, may also have roles in Drama Cast.*

Joseph-1: second in command of Egypt; speaks with confidence, authority, and genuine warmth; appears throughout musical (older child, youth, or adult)

Em-shee: female MC; speaks with confidence, energy, and expression; appears throughout musical (older child, youth, or adult)

Bilhah: guest speaker; Hebrew housekeeper from Joseph's youth; warm and friendly, possible solo (any age girl, youth, or adult)

Potiphar: guest speaker; Egyptian captain of the guard; sincere, speaks with authority (older girl or boy, youth, or adult; if girl, dress as male character)

Stew: guest speaker; Joseph's zany, Egyptian steward; full of life, speaks with enthusiasm and energy (any age boy or girl, youth, or adult)

Jacob: guest speaker; father of Joseph; warm and sincere (older boy, youth, or adult)

DRAMA CAST
(present scenes from Joseph's life)

Note: Drama Cast members, except Joseph-2, may play more than one role, if desired. The brother roles may be combined for fewer characters, or split to provide additional speaking roles. All roles may be played by boys, or girls dressed as male characters.

Pharaoh: speaks rhythmically, regally, and with authority; appears only in Drama 2 (older child, youth, or adult)

Cupbearer: speaks rhythmically, with expression; appears only in Drama 2 (any age)

Joseph-2: speaks rhythmically, with authority and expression; appears in Dramas 2, 3, and 4 (older child, youth, or adult)

Joseph's brothers: all speak with expression

Reuben*: speaks in Dramas 1 and 3 (any age)

Judah*: speaks in Dramas 1 and 4 (any age)

Simeon*: speaks only in Drama 3 (any age)

Benjamin*: appears and speaks only in Drama 4 (any age)

Brother 1: speaks in Dramas 1, 3, and 4 (any age)

Brother 2: speaks in Dramas 1 and 3 (any age)

*The name is given where dialogue from the Bible is attributed to a specific brother; otherwise, we have assigned numbers to them. You may name them, if desired. (See Genesis 35:23-26.)

ADDITIONAL ROLES:

Audience Prompters: cue audience response during designated songs
(2 to 6 boys or girls, any age)

Coat Carriers: short choreography with coat during "One Good
Lookin' Hebrew" (1 to 2 girls, any age)

Auction Bidders: 4 speaking bidders from audience for "Going, Going, Gone"
(adults or youth)

Nonspeaking bidders: as many as desired

NONSPEAKING ROLES:

sign bearers 1 to 4 children
brothers 2 to 6 children
additional brothers
optional attendants 2 to 4 children

SOLOS/ENSEMBLES

"One Good Lookin' Hebrew" Bilhah or other

"Going, Going, Gone" rhythmically speaking auctioneer; might be a speaking or
nonspeaking brother

"It's the Pits" solo stanza; optional ensemble

"Don't Wait! Don't Hesitate!" solo stanza; optional spoken ensemble

"I Forgive" Joseph-2 or other

"Our Mighty God" 1 to 4 solos

"I Just Want to Praise" 2 optional ensembles

COSTUMES AND PROPS

Everyone (choir, Stomp players, actors) could wear a basic Stomp costume, such as long, dark running pants with stripes down the side and T-shirts. Actors will add costume pieces to this basic uniform. These should be added onstage, before the audience. These costume pieces may be simple, such as a head covering and belt, to suggest the character being portrayed, or as elaborate as desired. Props and costumes could be placed on an onstage table or in various locations around the stage.

See Dovetailor for pictures of costumes and detailed suggestions for making them.

Joseph-1:	adds an Egyptian Pharaoh's headdress (a different color than the one worn by Pharaoh in Drama 2); wide gold collar/necklace and wide gold belt; also needs a long "coat of many colors" with long sleeves; may be worn open
Em-shee:	adds a red vest and red bow tie; holds a large book titled *Joseph, This Is Your Life*
Bilhah:	could wear a gray wig to appear elderly; adds a Hebrew* wrap or tunic; could have a cloth resembling an apron tied around her waist
Potiphar:	adds a ball cap worn backwards; cap should be painted gold and have a large medallion attached to the back of the cap (medallion should rest on the forehead when worn); wears a wide, V-shaped, brightly colored collar/necklace and a sash tied at the waist; a plastic sword or dagger could be tucked in the sash
Stew:	adds a pyramid-shaped hat or a jaw-length, white, Pharaoh-style headdress with a gold headband worn horizontally over it, gold armbands, and a large brightly striped "bib" with the letter "S" on it
Jacob:	adds a Hebrew* head covering, tunic or wrap, and belt; uses a walking stick
Pharaoh:	adds an Egyptian Pharaoh's headdress, wide gold collar/necklace, wide gold belt, and tall scepter

Cupbearer: adds a jaw-length, white, Pharaoh-style headdress with a gold headband worn horizontally over it, gold armbands, and wide sash; holds a tray with Pharaoh's cup glued to it

Joseph-2: might add a Hebrew* head covering and wrap or tunic in Drama 2; for fun, add black-and-white striped prison garb; adds Pharaoh-type attire matching Joseph-1 in all other dramas

Joseph's Brothers: all wear Hebrew* head coverings and varied colors of wraps or tunic pieces; some could carry shepherds' staffs, and some might have moneybags in their waistbands in Drama 1 (See Production Notes.); carry optional moneybags and large burlap drawstring bags, stuffed to appear full of grain in Scene 4; Benjamin carries Joseph's cup

Audience Prompters: could add brightly colored ball caps and gloves; could use 16- to 18-inch-long pieces of brightly colored foam, pool "noodles," or painted dowels as props for cuing audience (See Production Notes.)

Coat Carriers: add Hebrew* wrap or tunic and a head covering

Auction Bidders: wear present-day clothing; hold numbered bid paddles (See Production Notes for "Going, Going, Gone.")

Sign Bearers: could add colorful top hats (found at party stores); hold signs, which read: A Pitiful Situation, I've Got Good News and Bad News, Long Time No See, Show and Tell (See Dovetailor for sign design.)

Optional Attendants: dressed in Egyptian attire; could carry large palm fronds to fan Pharaoh

*Hebrew head covering could be a piece of fabric attached to a ball cap that is worn backwards. The tunic wrap could be a long piece of fabric worn behind the neck and hanging straight down in the front. Tie a rope or sash over it at the waist. (See Dovetailor.)

LIGHTING SUGGESTIONS

The lighting can be simple or elaborate.

Here are a few suggestions:
•During Dramas 1-4, lights could go to half on the *This Is Your Life* set and choir, leaving the drama area fully lit. This should occur after the sign carriers have crossed the stage.

•During "I Forgive," soft lighting could be used on the soloist. As the choir begins to sing, the lights should be brought up.

SET DESIGN

The sets may be simple or elaborate.

Stage Right (*This Is Your Life* set)

This set should have a backdrop with "Joseph, This Is Your Life" written in large, bright, readable letters. For fun, consider using a sign with marquee lights. The backdrop might be a screen, freestanding wall, or curtain. Ensure that it does not block the audience's sight line of the choir. There should be a "chair of honor" for Joseph in front of the backdrop. This could simply be a pastor's chair or a decorative chair, resembling a throne. Elevate the chair on a small platform. Em-shee should have a stool to sit on when not delivering dialogue. There could also be a small table or podium. "Dress up" this area with helium balloons or plants.

Dramas 1-4 take place center stage and do not require a set. Props and costume pieces should be onstage on low tables or placed around the stage.

Stage Left (Stomp Band area)

Attach metal stomp instruments on a large section of chain-link fence or a wall. (If using a wall, check the sight line of the audience.) This area should be visually exciting and fun. Consider using Egyptian-style graffiti. (See Dovetailor for suggestions.) All stomp instruments may be in this area, or some may be stage right. Ladders could be upstage right and left.

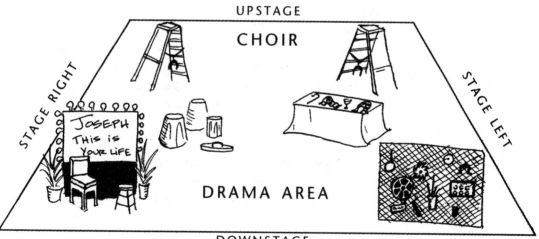

PRODUCTION NOTES

•See the Dovetailor and demonstration video for detailed information and demonstrations of stomp choreography, costuming, set, and props.

•General stage directions are included in the script.

•In the script, everyone refers to all onstage choir and stomp players.

•Actors will add "costume pieces" to their basic stomp uniform. These should be added onstage, before the audience, prior to their drama segment.

•Throughout the musical, Em-shee and Joseph-1 listen and watch as guests speak, songs are performed, and dramas are presented. Em-shee may sit on the stool during songs and dramas, but should stand when speaking to Joseph-1, who remains seated, unless otherwise noted.

•When *This Is Your Life* guests enter, they should deliver their lines slightly stage left of the *This Is Your Life* set.

•There are several instances where audience participation will add to the fun. Audience PowerPoint® cues are included on the Enhanced Listening CD. Other options are to use handheld signs or to print song lyrics in the program.

Opening Commentary:
•As stomp players and choir members take their places, the atmosphere is upbeat and excited, with lots of smiling faces. When Em-shee and Joseph-1 move downstage for their opening lines, everyone should watch them, focus on what they say, and cheer and applaud as indicated. The track should begin immediately after the final dialogue is spoken.

"Joseph: From the Pit to the Palace"
•As meas. 22 is sung, the Audience Prompters move downstage to direct the audience in their "Joseph" responses and hand claps on the "Celebrate tonight" sections. Audience cues should also appear on PowerPoint® or handheld signs.

•When Em-shee and Joseph-1 are seated on the *This Is Your Life* set, they listen and watch as the song is performed.

•At the end of the song, prompters or other children might throw streamers and confetti from the front of the stage.

DRAMA 1

•Ten brothers may be included in this scene. They should stand in conversational clusters. To add visual variety, brothers without speaking parts could kneel on one knee or sit on an overturned bucket.

•If there are several optional persons in this scene, some may exit with Reuben and Brother 1.

"Going, Going, Gone"

•Shepherds' staffs and moneybags are used as Stomp instruments. These Stomp players could play the roles of brothers in Drama 1, or different players could come to center stage to play the Stomp parts.

•The Auctioneer may be a brother or someone else that moves downstage center to speak to the audience.

•Prearranged auction bids should be voiced from the audience. Bidders should have bid paddles with numbers and stand when they speak. Bidders may choose their own bid wording. For added atmosphere, have other persons raise and wave their bid paddles, without speaking. Schedule time for the speaking bidders to practice this song with the choir before the program.

DRAMA 2

•Optional attendants could carry large palm fronds for fanning Pharaoh. They could gently fan as they take their places but should hold the palm fronds still once the dialogue begins. This is also applicable in Dramas 3 and 4.

"It's Not About Me"

•Optional: This would be a fun audience participation song. The audience might sing the final repeat of the chorus, meas. 28-67. These word cues should appear on PowerPoint® or handheld signs. Audience prompters could cue audience participation, then signal them to stop by crossing their sticks to form an X, then turning toward the choir and pointing at them, or they might hold up a STOP sign.

DRAMA 3

•In Dramas 3 and 4, Joseph-2 delivers asides directly to the audience. When this occurs, all Drama Cast members should freeze as Joseph-2 takes a couple of steps toward the audience and speaks. After he speaks, Joseph-2 rejoins the Drama Cast, they unfreeze, and the drama continues as if uninterrupted.

Stew—"Operation Bring 'Em Back"
•Stew asks the audience four questions. The audience, choir, etc. will respond with a rousing "Yes!" to each one. Stew should motion, hands extended toward audience, for their response. Cues also appear on PowerPoint® or handheld signs. Audience prompters could cue audience.

DRAMA 4
•When brothers enter, they should be obviously distraught, scared, and apprehensive. Brothers should avoid standing in a straight line across the stage. After the brothers bow, they could leave their "grain" bags on the floor.

•After Joseph reveals his identity to the brothers, they should gather in a semicircle around him as they deliver their lines. The sight line between the audience and Joseph should be clear.

"Our Mighty God"
•Optional: The audience could join in singing the chorus at meas. 98-109. These word cues should appear on PowerPoint®. Audience prompters could cue audience participation and signal them to stop.

"I Just Want to Praise"
•This closing song is upbeat and energetic. Depending on your choreography, you could fill the stage with actors, Stomp players, etc. in all-out praise and celebration.
•Optional: The audience could join in praise for meas. 78-84.

STOMP SUGGESTIONS

•HAVE FUN! That is the number one thing!

•Stomp as simply or elaborately as desired. The suggested rhythm patterns may be simplified or expanded to meet your group's needs.

•All instruments can play the same pattern, or different types of instruments can play during different sections. It will sound great even if you do a simple Stomp because the tracks are full of rhythm.

•Any object can become a Stomp instrument, so feel free to substitute instruments. Be creative and adventurous! Experiment with different objects and various strikers to discover sounds that work best in your auditorium. The Stomp instruments we used are listed and described on the Listening CD.

•If multiples of the instruments are played, do not overpower the singers.

•Share the fun! If you have numerous kids who want to play Stomp instruments, assign them different songs to accompany.

•Stomp players may remain stage right or left, or some might come to center stage to be featured during appropriate places in the songs. See the Dovetailor and demonstration video for detailed performance suggestions and a demonstration of Stomp choreography.

•Stomp rhythm patterns for the songs are provided on the Accompaniment CD (ACD). When the ACD is inserted in a computer, a disk icon appears. When opened, the rhythm patterns for the songs may be printed. A list of Stomp instruments used on the recording are also included.

SUGGESTIONS FOR TEACHING STOMP

•Teach the words of the songs first. This will help Stomp players know when to play.

•The players will be most successful if they learn the rhythm patterns while hearing how they fit together with other patterns. Introduce each pattern separately. Follow these simple steps:

°Without instruments, all players learn the first rhythm pattern. They should continue clapping or tapping the pattern until all are confident. Speaking words to a pattern often makes it easier to recall (for example, "Praise the Lord").

°As players continue performing the first pattern, you play the second pattern. Continue for several repetitions so they can hear the sound of the patterns together.

°Teach players the second pattern. Split the group in half, and let them play the two patterns together.

°Introduce each new pattern this way. When mastered, transfer patterns to instruments.

Joseph:
FROM THE PIT TO THE PALACE
<u>DOVETAILOR!</u>

DON'T MISS the opportunity to teach spiritual truths as the children learn the musical! Fun activities are included for each week's rehearsal that guide the children in applying the spiritual truths presented in the songs and dialogue. Opportunities are also presented for Scripture memorization.

DON'T MISS the opportunity to teach the children about music! Fun games and activities are incorporated into each weekly rehearsal to help the children learn about music.

DON'T MISS the opportunity to save hours of planning! A schedule is included that takes you from the enrollment party to the night of the program. It lists the tasks that need to be completed each week for a stress-free musical.

DON'T MISS 12 weeks of rehearsal plans! Each week, simply take the Rehearsal Plan and activities out of the notebook and you're ready for a fun, action-packed, productive rehearsal. You'll find a well-planned rehearsal, detailing the song sections to teach, and the related musical and spiritual activities. The rehearsal will contain large-group time, the option of small groups, and opportunities for the children to move, sing, and play instruments.

DON'T MISS the Teaching Notes! Each song is divided into teachable segments with suggestions for teaching them in a fun, efficient manner. The segments are referenced on the weekly Rehearsal Plans.

DON'T MISS the Production Notes! They are packed with instructions for making sets, props, costumes, and lighting. They also include Suggested Audition Readings, Audition Rating Sheets, Casting Records, Stomp Teaching Suggestions, and much more.

DON'T MISS the Enrollment Party Plans! These plans include everything from the invitation and enrollment forms, to food and game suggestions. Exciting, colorful posters and clip art are also included. All the work is done for you!

DON'T MISS IT!

Other products from
JIMMY AND GAIL

Christmas Shorts

Unison/Easy/Three 12-minute shorts or one 40-minute musical

It's three Christmas musicals in one! Yes, this dynamic musical for children offers three 12-minute miniprograms—each of which is packed with clever drama and fun songs—that can be presented individually or combined for a full-length, 40-minute performance. These zany programs can be performed in any combination, linked with dialogue between a grandmother and granddaughter as they open holiday mail and share Christmas cards.

Titles: A Christmas Parade: It's a Parade; Christmas in America; Carol Medley; It's a Parade (Reprise); From Our Herd to Your Herd, Merry Christmas!: Good News, Wonderful News; A Shepherd's Heart; From Our Herd to Your Herd, Merry Christmas!; An ADVENTurous Christmas: Have an ADVENTurous Christmas; Light the Candles of Advent; The Gift Rappers; The Candle of Christ; Have an ADVENTurous Christmas (Reprise)

The Good News Christmas Cruise

Unison & 2-part/Easy/35 minutes

The passengers and crew of the SS Good News are excited about their upcoming celebration with the people of Laruba, to whom they will present a beautiful mission bell. But first, the passengers and crew perform a play titled "The Promise" for their guests. Through moving drama and upbeat songs, this presentation traces God's promise to send a Savior to the world.

Titles: The Good News Christmas Cruise; Super Spectaculous, Grand and Miraculous; Come to Me; Deck the Deck; Christmas Is All About Love; Abra, Abra, Abraham; Keep Watching, Keep Waiting; Carol Medley (Silent Night, Holy Night/O Little Town of Bethlehem/The First Noel/O Come, All Ye Faithful); The Promise; Come to Me (Reprise); Good News Christmas Cruise (Reprise)

The Good News Cruise

Unison & 2-part/Easy/40 minutes

Pull up the gangway, blow the horn, it's time to sail, so all on board! Come join us on the SS Good News for a joyous, fun-filled cruise! In this delightful musical for children, events and activities onboard ship are used to explore, explain, and celebrate the abundant life found only in Jesus Christ.

Titles: The Good News Cruise; We Are Servants of the Lord; Soakin' Up the Son; Bible, Prayer, and the Holy Spirit; This Boat Is Rockin'; For You Are God; The Great Commission; Got Jesus?; Lost and Found; Welcome to the Family of God; Celebrate Jesus; Good News Cruise Finale

Kings, Dreams, and Schemes

Unison & 2-part/Easy/35 minutes

Gathered around a computer screen, an inquisitive bunch of kids pop a new computer CD into the drive for Kings, Dreams, and Schemes, where they see Daniel's life of obedience unfold. As they watch the screen, the stories are performed by another drama group, and the choir tells the tale through song of Daniel's awesome victory!

Titles: Kings, Dreams, and Schemes; We Can't Eat the King's Choice Food; The King Had a Dream; Another Dream; You Can't Top the Power of God; The Handwriting on the Wall; Three Times a Day; They Threw Daniel in the Lion's Den; Glory to the God of Daniel; Dare to Be a Daniel

The Plane Truth About Christmas

Arranged by Barny Robertson
Unison & 2-part/Easy/40 minutes

In this easy and fun-to-learn musical for children in grades 1–6, a family stranded in the O'Hare Airport decides to share their faith with other travelers through a mini Christmas pageant.
Titles: It's Christmas Time!; Nana Rap; No Fair! O'Hare, No Fair!; His Name Is Jesus; Jesus Is the Reason for the Season; The Plane Truth About Christmas; An Angel Came to Mary; No Fair! Caesar, No Fair!; Step by Step (Walking to Bethlehem); Hey, You! Keeper of the Ewes; Silent Night, Holy Night; What Makes a Wise Man Wise/O Come, All Ye Faithful; It's Christmas Time!/ The Plane Truth (Finale)

Stomp and Praise

3 Songs of Praise with "Stomp" Instrumentation
Unison/Easy

Stomp, bang, hammer, clap, and praise the Lord! That's the terrific idea behind *Stomp and Praise,* a children's collection that kids are gonna go wild over!

This exciting new praise experience combines Scripture-based songs with "Stomp" instrument accompaniment! Children can use just about anything that makes a sound to play the unique rhythm patterns provided for each song. Rhythm charts may be printed from the enhanced listening CD. No matter who plays what, you'll get fun, funky songs that will tap, bang, and plop seeds of biblical truth into the hearts of children.